Chinese Thunder Magic

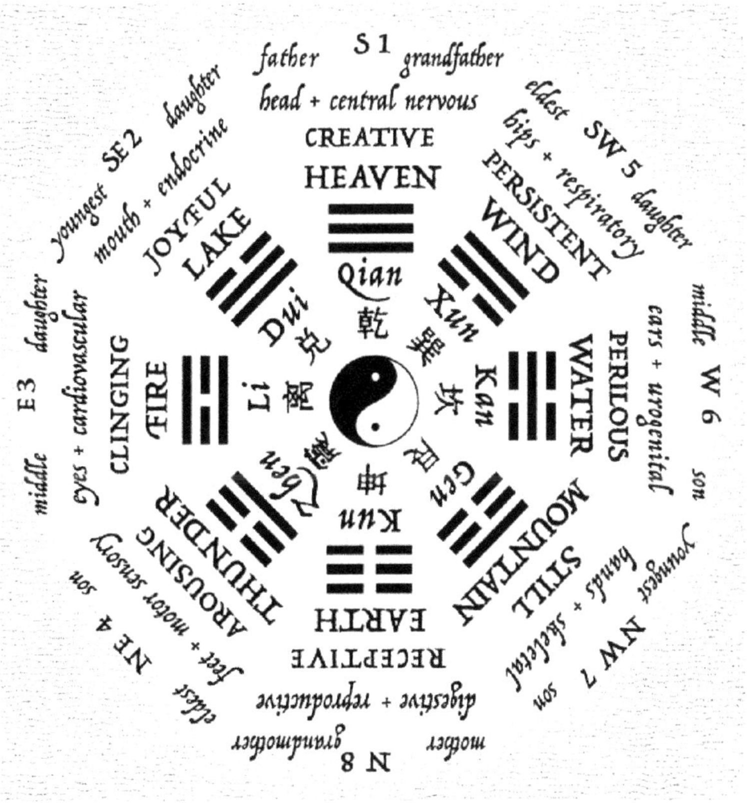

© Jason Read 2021
First Edition

All rights reserved. No part of this work may be reproduced, stored in a retrieval system, or transmitted in any form or by any means, electronic, mechanical, photocopying, recording or otherwise without the prior permission of the publisher.

The methodologies in this book stem from the author's own experiences. The Reader must not regard the information as an alternative to medical advice, which he should obtain from a qualified professional. The Reader who thinks he might be suffering from a medical condition should seek medical advice immediately. The Reader who is already in receipt of medical treatment should not discontinue or delay this treatment or disregard medical advice as a consequence of having read the information in this book. The author and the publishers cannot accept legal responsibility for any problem arising out of experimenting with the methods described.

Chinese Thunder Magic

Jason Read

Marshal Peng

Contents

The Chinese Magick Series 7
Thunder Magic 9

Part One Cultivation Of Maoshan Thunder Palm 11

Basic Principles 11
Maoshan Lei Fa Mi Zhi
(The Secret Decree Of Maoshan Thunder Law) 12
Preparatory Practice 13
Practice of the Thunder Power 17
Afternotes 24

Part Two Testing the Thunder Palm 25

Cai Ju Leidian Fa
(The Method Of Gathering
The Thunder And Lightning Power) 26
The Five Thunder Hand Seal 28
The Exorcism By Thunder 30

Zhuo Fa Shu
(The Skill Of Magical Capturing) 33
Introducing the Basic Thunder Symbols 35
Steps to creating the Thunder Seal 38
Five Thunder Lock Talisman 40
A Thunder Method To Treat Pain 42
The Thunder Pouch 44
The Technique Of The Substitute Grass Puppet 44
The Quick Thunder Palm Method 47
Five Thunder Talismans 48

1. Wu Lei Zhou
(Five Thunder Spell) 49
The Fire Of The Five Thunders
Or The So Called Samadhi Fire 58
The Samadhi Fire Spell 60

Glossary 63

The Chinese Magick Series

The mysteries of Chinese occultism have long been hidden from the West, largely due to the cultural and language barriers between us. Also because of the reluctance of the Chinese Masters to part with their knowledge.

For this reason we are producing this series of books to fill that gap in the knowledge of most western magicians. This knowledge comes from both oral and written sources that can only be found in Chinese communities. The author has travelled extensively in China and Malaysia and personally learned under several teachers from a school of practical magic known as Maoshan.

Maoshan is a school of magic dealing with the interaction of the seen and unseen worlds, with a knowledge base dating back thousands of years to the time of the ancient shaman kings who ruled that area of China known as the Sichuan Plateau. Over many generations the Maoshan school developed hundreds if not thousands of unique techniques to alleviate the challenges of life as well as to explore our spiritual nature and that of the cosmos.

Maoshan, the school devoted to practical magic is unveiled in these books for the first time in the English language. We hope this opens a door to the mysterious world of the ancient chinese sorcerers. Forthcoming volumes include:

Thunder Magic.
Secrets of Chinese necromancy.
Chinese love and sex magic and alchemy.
Mysteries of Chinese Star magick.
Chinese talismanic Magick.

The Book of the Nine Tailed Fox.
Chinese Magickal Healing and Rejuvenation.
Chinese Magick of Fortune and Gambling.
The Training of a Chinese Sorcerer.
Chinese Magical Defence and Attack.

Thunder Magic

The art of thunder magic, or as it is known in Taoism, Lei Fa the Thunder Law or the Thunder Method is one of the principle techniques learned in Maoshan occultism. It has its own set of techniques and talismans, coupled with training techniques that should be mastered by the apprentice of the Maoshan Pai (School).

Some would argue that the Thunder Law is the mighty Lord of all the inner strength techniques of Tao magic, at least of all the Yang orientated techniques. The techniques of Thunder Law have been passed down by oral tradition for centuries, since the Song Dynasty magician Lin Lingsu. Thunder magic soon caught on as the primary technique of the Masters. The tradition was developed by Wang Wen Jing, Bai Yu Chan and Huang Shu Shen in the 12th and 13th centuries, mainly in the Celestial Master Schools.

Over time and with the rise and fall of kingdoms they have become rather staid ineffective ritual curiosities in the hands of the orthodox schools, but the technique also passed into the hands of the folk sorcerers including Maoshan Pai, and thus the real power was not lost or merely a fossilized ritual curiosity.

Bai Yu Chan. Ancestor of the Thunder Law

Part One Cultivation Of Maoshan Thunder Palm Basic Principles

1. It is a mistake to think that Lei Fa is actual power over thunder and storms, though with great masters this could happen. In fact the thunder power is a symbolic representation of the transmission of the Yang energies from Heaven to Earth. Thunder and lightning is merely a symbolic representation of that power of the action between the Heavens and the Earth. However as noted before there is a correlation between the physical storm and the powers cultivated by the Maoshan magician. But that need not concern us here yet.

2. It will suffice us to say that the Thunder power is an internalised power originating from the tremendous energies that interact from Heaven and Earth.

3. In training this fa gong (Skill in Method) you should be meticulous in every step and be patient.

4. The method is used for self-defense, the elimination of evil, disintegrating ghosts and demons, protecting homes....for example by clearing away xie, or unhealthy environmental qi miasma, and finally at a very last resort for punishing. Thus it can also be used for healing and destruction. If successfully cultivated, you should be very cautious.

4. Everyone can try but not all will be successful due to the matter of destiny. You may or may not be ready. It cannot be forced without great danger. Those of a wood nature should be careful. Look at your hands. If they have obvious knots like bamboo stems observe extreme caution.

Maoshan Lei Fa Mi Zhi (The Secret Decree Of Maoshan Thunder Law)

I am Spirit, the Law is good. If I am not good, how can the Thunder Lords listen to me? If I am good, the Thunder Gods respond. If I feel the divinity in myself, the Gods are not careless in working through me. I am as a God, nothing is fruitless and there is no delusion. The heart is true and the heart is one with the Thunder Gods. I am a Thunder God, and the Thunder God is me. Acting by the Will of Heaven and Earth I cannot err.

5. There are taboos that one must observe while engaging in the Thunder Arts. Do not think you cannot obey them or ignore them as some kind of irrelevant vestige of older times. You must for the period of training engage in the full practice and be mindful of the taboos of practice.

    a. You cannot pass to the unfaithful. The non-believing, the unfilial or unrighteous.

    b. You cannot teach one who has 'bamboo' like knots in their hands as they can easily be struck by lightning.

    c. You cannot eat beef, dog, rabbit, snake or have sex during the training. If the student is quick of intellect you will realize that essentially you cannot eat the sacred animals of the Earthly Branches for energetic reasons. Also the command not to have sex is not some moralistic adjunct but merely to build up magical energies.

Preparatory Practice

1. Obtain or make an image of Taishang Laojun. If you are not familiar with him, he is one of the Three Pure Ones (San Qing) and the essence of the teaching ray that emanated wisdom teachings to this world. His most familiar incarnations are Fu Xi and Lao Zi. So in other words he is the spiritual form and essence of the earthly teacher we call LaoZi..

2. You must arrange a practice room that we call the Room of Solitude or Silence (Jing Shinei). Use a compass or luopan to find North. And hang or stand the picture in that direction.

3. Sit before the picture, clear your mind, relax. Focus on the image of Taishang Laojun for a while. Then close your eyes and retain his form (xing) in your mind. This mental image of Lord Lao must still seem to be on the outside. A real presence before you, not merely an image in your mind, but there, physically in space. Make it lifelike as possible, even the radiant body heat and smell...say of jasmine flowers. Practice this until the image of Laojun seems three dimensional and concrete in the space before you. You should be able to 'conjure' this before you at will. With practice it will become more and more solid. You could compare this process to the Tibetan Yidam practice. Do not proceed until you can do this to your Shifu's satisfaction. Such production of mental thought-forms are vital to the successful practice of Taoist magic.

4. You should now obtain three red apples and place in a porcelain dish of the finest quality. Place on a table, which is to the North under the Icon of Taishang Laojun. The plate should be placed on a round red cloth

5. Add to the Altar (tan) three bowls of Law Water in three half filled small bowls, arranging them in a triangle. Around the bowl of apples, to the North, East and the West.

6. The offerings should be replaced every three days at most when engaging in the Lei Fa practice. You may eat the fruit but it is taboo to give them to those outside Maoshan. When the day's practice is over, you can throw the water away in the direction of the Sun. The water is changed and thrown daily.

7. An incense pot is placed in front of the plate of apples i.e. to the South Inside is a half cup of rice to which you can mix salt if you wish. Arrange three ancient style Chinese coins in a triangle on the top of the rice. Each time you are cultivating Thunder, burn three incense sticks. Inserting them through the square holes of the coins into the rice.

8. Another option, but one requiring more courage and riskier in this modern age, is to practice in a cemetery. Ideally you will find the grave of one who has been struck by lightning...that is easier than you think in this day and age of information. One faces the grave, burns the incense and burns 7 sheets of silver spirit money. Then light firecrackers to the west.

9. Buy a new Chinese style brush pen, a glass of Chinese rice wine or Bai Jiu, some cinnabar and a little white wheat (bai mai). Boil the white wheat until you see white glutinous juice and bottle it up for later use. Furthermore you boil 12 grains of white rice in water in a clean iron pan, strain it to make rice water (Young rice is best for this). Mix the cinnabar with the rice water and add three drops of white wheat worter and white rice wine. Put in a bottle and shake to mix it well.

10. It should be noted that cinnabar has a very long history in Chinese occultism and alchemy. However I must warn the reader that it is toxic in nature and has risks. It would be wise to replace cinnabar with some other red pigment. Red ochre is a good choice as is dragon's blood resin.

11. The best times to train are at the Jiazi days rather than the

Thunder Magick ☙ 15

Taishang Laojun

Ding days.. The First and Fifteenth days of the Lunar Calendar are also well. That would be the New Moon and the Full Moon. Any positive Taoist Festival is good, such as the Dragon Boat Day is especially auspicious.

12. The preferred hours of cultivation are Zi Shi and Yinshi. (11pm-1am) (3am-5 am).
13. Three days before practice begin fasting. No wine or meat but vegetables, fruits, pulses and grains are ok. Bathe and brush teeth before practice.

Practice of the Thunder Power

1. At the Altar light three sticks of incense and insert into the Incense Pot. Place palms together before the chest and recite the first spell thus:

   Qing SanQing San Jing Taishang Laojun, Lei Shen Dadi, Jiu Tian Xuan Nu, qi qu Wen Chang Xing Jun, Zhen mo ling gong dajiang yu xian taohua sheng xiang, Beidou zi guang furen Zi jin, Furen fan Gua Jin tong bao gua Yunu hua fu xian shi zhang Tianshi shi Sandai yao wang mingyi gu xian shi yang gong lai gong liu an Difu Yanjun zhi nian da Suijing Jun Yinyang er jiao zhuban shenling zushi enshi shi bo shi shu shixiong shidi shijie shimei qianqian bingma baiwan shen jiang dizi pai ming buzhou biao ming bujin zi guang ling qi hujia xiangyun qing jiang xiang tan dizi qian cheng dingli cifu xian ling zuo zheng.

   (I ask of you O three Pure Ones and the Three Realms, and you O Master Taishang Laojun, The Mighty Great Thunder Lord God, and you the Mysterious Girl of the Nine Heavens, the Seven Qu Wen Chang Star King, guarding the hall/room from evil spirits, the Jade General, the Peach Blossom Sage, the purple light rays of the Big Dipper Great Lady, The Purple Metal Lady Gua, the Metal Child who declares the oracles, the Jade Maiden who draws the magical figures, the Elder Teacher who reveals the Heavenly Teacher, the Thirty Generations of Medicine Kings, famed doctors, the Ghost Valley Ancestor Teacher Yang, the Three Palaces, the Six Tables of the Underworld, Yanjun, Lord of Hell, the Yearly Great Star of the Year King, Yin and Yang, the two teachers, and all the many divinities and ancestral founders, teachers, eldest brother teachers, youngest brother teachers, junior male teachers and senior male teachers, senior female and junior sister teachers, the thousand upon thousands of troops and their steeds, the millions of gods assist me, the disciple, forgive my errors and carelessness. The purple light, the spiritual qi reaches the Emperor on auspicious clouds, descend on the sweet cloud to this altar, to your devout disciple who bows before you , and bless me in the presence of your manifest power and witness my righteousness.)

2. The above should be written on yellow paper before the ritual begins. Keep it on the altar for ease of reading. You can write in Chinese (best) or in English. On the final day of finishing the practice you burn it and thank the teacher.

3. Now pick up the brush pen (maobi) and load with cinnabar ink (zhusha), or use the right hand in the sword finger hand seal and write the Thunder Talisman on the index, middle, ring and little fingers of the left hand..

4. Once the symbol has been drawn, put the brush down and sit down in your chosen posture about two feet away from the altar.

5. Now the palm and fingers must be kept straight and inline with the root of the thumb. Lay the hand on the flat surface of the altar table so the middle finger is pointing directly at the bowl of water in the North. Do not be tense, relax so the joints of the arm sink towards the ground. The right hand in the meantime is relaxed naturally on your lap. Relax, be mindful.

Thunder Magick ⋈ 19

Image of basic Thunder Cultivation. Above you can see the Thunder Seal to be drawn on the fingers.

6. When you feel you have entered a clear state of mind and you feel ready, close your eyes. Then imagine coalescing before you, the Lord Taishang Laojun. Taishang Laojun should be there before you as real looking as possible with every detail as you practiced before in the preliminary practice.

7. Now the image and therefore the presence of Laojun being 'fixed' before you, you must, in your heart relate to yourself the following line of thought, if it helps you can say this not only mentally but in a low voice. Feel these words, contemplate them and make them part of your reality.

   Taishang Laojun is the Supreme Ancestor in whom I sincerely believe. The Tao is my path. I accept the path of the Tao fully in my life. I shall cultivate the Five Thunder Law and I resolve to succeed. I have made up my mind to be assiduous and diligent in my practice. I shall do good deeds and avoid evil. I earnestly request Taishang Laojun, the Great Ancestor of the Daojia to bestow and confer upon me the ancient skill. So be it.

8. Now you must perform the 'Transform into a God Spell'. The spell is said three times as follows:

   Lei Shen jiang hua qian zhen ling wu dizi he zhen xing taishang jinkou xiang chuanshou jiao wu shen wai geng shengshen.

   (O the Thunder Lord will assist the true transformation of I the disciple, joining the disciple with the true form and teaching through the golden mouth the transformation of my parent-born body!)

9. Now close your eyes and look within your heart and visualise a pink lotus flower. This should be in the centre of the chest at the shanzhong Point. Focus your mind on the flower for some moments so you can even feel its weight and detect its sweet smell. Now watch the petals open and unfold one by one, to reveal the yellow stamens and centre.

On the centre is sat a child of around six years old. Again make this real and as three dimensional as possible.

10. The lotus descends down the centre of your body to the dantian. You should know that this point is about an inch and a half below your navel.. Remember this is in, within your body's centre, not on the surface of your skin. Once the Lotus and Child have settled there at the dantian you must imagine that child growing into a man before your very eyes. Growing into one the form of the Thunder God you have chosen. Say the mantra as you do this:

    Wo ji Lei Shen, Lei Shen ji wo.'

    (I am the Thunder Spirit, the Thunder Spirit is me).

11. Now conjure Taishang Laojun before you again, the image as before, but then imagine yourself transforming into one of the Thunder Lords. Laojun still before you. This should be intense and real as possible to every sense. You may choose any of the Thunder Gods, some of which are pictured in this lesson booklet.. When you feel at one and merged with the Thunder God, you are to lick the Thunder Talisman off your fingers. Begin at the index, then middle, ring and little fingers, one by one. Close one only eye through all this process. The Thunder Talisman is mixed with your saliva and then you swallow it.

12. Once you finish this process, mentally thank the Dao Ancestors for their assistance, Then slowly let the Thunder God form you have assumed shrink and retrace its steps back to the lotus child form. Be meticulous and do not rush this process!

14. Once back to the child form, allow the petals to close one by one so you are back to a lotus bud.

15. The lotus now suddenly bursts into fame to become a sphere of hot iridescent red light. Again this must be clearly not just

visualized but FELT, and in three dimensions at the dantian. With practice this will actually warm you up even on a cold day!

16. Make the Five Thunders Hand Seal (this is the double version as shown in the picture), and hold around 10 centimeters from the dantian. Then utter the spell as you hold the Five Thunders Hand Seal (Wu Lei Jue):

Dianguang, dianguang chuzi Kan fang, pan huo wanli shang zhi Tiantang, wu fang Di chi shou fu xin Wang. Ji ji ru dianguang.

Lightning ! Lightning ! Comes from the Kan power, emanating fire over thousands of miles and ascending to the paradise of Heaven, by the Powerful Emperor's command and Lord of my heart! As quick as Lightning!

16. Let the mantric spell vibrate through the body and the left hand, you must simultaneously visualize that the hands are shining and hot and emitting thunder and lightning. To your mind, everything is disappearing except the hand and the Dantian. Practice this for at least 3 to 5 minutes.

17. Now inhale slowly and deeply through the nose with a natural breathing pattern. This means that when you inhale the diaphragm and abdomen are pushed NATURALLY (do not force it with tension) outwards. When you exhale the abdomen comes in, again without tension. As you inhale you visualize the thunder and lightning emanating from your hands following the stream of your breath into your nose and down through the central channel into your Dantian, which, remember, is still the sphere of compacted red fiery energy.

Practice this Thunder Breath at least five times but the more the better. Always use odd numbers of breaths.

18. Then both hands lower to the sides of the body with palms down and arms at right angles. The fingers face forwards.

Inhale and lift the palms upwards. Move them up and down vertically, breathing a few times. Finally hit the ground quickly and hard as you mentally say:

Dianshan Leiming Shanbeng Dilie!!

Lightning Flashes Thunder Shakes Mountains And Earth.

Repeat this 49 times, trying to hold your breath.. Practice with one or two palms at your preference. You can do the lifting and lowering palms breathing between rounds of strikes.

19. You can also practice standing up, preferably in Horse Stance (ma bu) to practice the strikes on wood, paper, sand bags or whatever you choose to use. Even the air is acceptable.

    When inhaling, stand in a natural Wuji Stance and inhale as you raise hands to above head and lower them when exhaling. When hands lower guide the Qi to the Dantian.

    Practice this 3 to 7 times.

20. Finally, whether seated or standing, put your hands together in front of the body as in praying and thank the Master. Burn three sheets of yellow paper or spirit money before you on the ground.

21. Continue this process for 21 to 49 days. If you repeat this cycle after 49 days to build more powerful thunder energy or because you were interrupted, take 2 to 3 days off and then repeat.

Afternotes

All things reflect Tai Chi and so too, the human body is Tai Chi. The left side of the body is Yang, and the right side of the body is Yin. The five fingers correspond to the Wuzang or Five Internal Organs...Heart, Liver, Spleen, Lungs and the Kidneys, the Five Directions and the Elements and so on. Thus the Taoist scholars say that the hand contains all dharmas.

Each day you should practice only once, and every evening the water on the altar should be changed.

If you practice more than once a day you can hurt yourself. The results of this method for some students can be very fast.

You may also hear strange noises in the house as you practice but do not worry as this is quite normal. Stay calm and think of positive and righteous thoughts.

Another thing you may notice is that the body seems to swell slightly as the qi and blood surge through the body.

Some students may see ghosts or demons and other disturbing scenes during this cultivation method. This means that the Yin Qi in your body is in excess. You should stop practice and accumulate merit through good works, neigong and scriptural study and only then try again.

If you do encounter a demon as you cultivate, recall the image of Taishang Laojun and he will soon disappear.

Do not tell people that you are cultivating this method except others in the Maoshan School, such as your teacher or fellow disciples.

To reveal that you are cultivating is to leak power.

Part Two
Testing the Thunder Palm

After seven days, or if you are slower in development, whenever you feel ready, you can proceed to testing the validity of the thunder palm.

Firstly you should get a paper cup or carton, small in size, then catch a fly, ant or some other insect. Catch it and put it in the carton or cup and obviously cover it so the insect doesn't escape. Place it on the altar.

Now visualise that you have become the Thunder God in the usual method. Then strike or wave your 'thunder charged' palm over the cup seven times willing thunder power.

You may notice the insect responding. If your power is strong the insect is instantly killed. If this occurs your cultivation is excellent. If nothing happens, just continue to practice until results come. Try around every seven days.

Fate and the kindness of the Immortal Masters will help you gain the skill if you are moral and wise. It cannot be forced. If you do force it and you succeed, beware of the consequences.

Cai Ju Leidian Fa
(The Method Of Gathering The Thunder And Lightning Power)

This method is best done in the Spring, waiting for the Spring rains and thunderstorms. However this method can be used whenever there is a storm. We must remember that the method was developed in southern China by our Maoshan ancestors. In Spring at the time known as Qianhou or the 'Awakening of Insects', most Chinese eagerly awaited the first rains and storms that signaled the end of the unproductive winter. However you must take into account your own geographical location AND take advantage of any storm power that may be around.

When you feel or know a storm is coming (how lucky we have weather forecasts in this day and age!), you should go to your quiet room and light three sticks of incense.

Now stand in the Taoist magical posture known as Dingzi Bu or Ding Character Stance. This is where your feet are in the position of a T shape. Face the direction of the thunder and the storm and hold the Five Thunder Hand Seal with your left hand as shown. Then recite the following mantric spell silently:

Shang Tianci wo wei zhen wan ling Di jiang zhenlei ru wu fu sheng, gui wen nao lie chuyu jing shen ji ji ru lu ling!!!!

(Heaven bestows on me the Zhen thunder, ten thousand spirits descending to the Earth, the resonant Zhen Thunder enters my belly and the ghosts hear and their minds break and they cry in fear, Gods quickly by Law!!)

In your mind think of the thunder shaking power of Zhen, and the Thunder Qi is as a luminous mist or gas. As you inhale, draw that Thunder mist through the nose or mouth and 'swallow' (tunyan) so it passes down the central meridian and into your dantian. Repeat this seven times. Reach 24 cycles.

In the belly there builds in your mind's eye, the scintillating and crackling electrical and fiery, raging flames.

This gathers thunder power can be stored for later use.

You can use it to charge talismans or exorcise Yin spirits for example. You literally lead the thunder fire up through the palm and 'spray' the fire into the talisman.

The Five Thunder Hand Seal

The little, ring and middle fingers of the left hand grasp the index and ring fingers of the right hand. Five fingers stick out to represent the five thunders.

You can use the Thunder Symbol as you drew it on your palm earlier or in conjunction with any of the Thunder Talismans and rites to be taught later in this booklet.

Holding the left hand in thunder and having performed seven to twenty four thunder breaths, chant the spell:

Dian huo dianguang chuzi nanfang yi huo wanli shang dao tiantang , wu feng Di chi shou fu xin wang! Ji ji ru luling!!!

Lightning Fire, Lightning Light coming from the South, Miracle Fire over a thousand miles reaching and soaring to Heaven, I honour the Supreme Emperor and receive Him as the Lord of my Heart! Quickly by Law!

Again, breathe 7 to 24 thunder breaths deep into the dantian in the belly and ponder that power as filling your body till your eyes flash with electrical thunder qi and shoot it into the talisman.

Be cautious when practicing this method. Never ever do it in the open, under the outer eaves of your home or under trees for obvious reasons.

There may be times when a storm comes, but you haven't had time to prepare, say for example you don't have incense and you're not in your altar room. It's ok. Focus on the storm and do as much as you can using the breathing of storm essence and the spell. Remember to start inhaling at every flash of lightning to 'catch the thunder mist/essence', Keep the eyes wide open and show courtesy to Heaven and the Dao Ancestors.

These are the basic skills then, of gaining the thunder palm and its power, which can be further supplemented with the Gathering the Thunder Method. In fact the Gathering of the Thunder Method can be used alone without the Thunder Palm cultivation by those not wanting that skill. However both skills are essential skills to the Maoshan magician.

There are further, more advanced cultivation methods that we shall look at later, but the Thunder Palm and the Gathering the Thunder are the basics that give you a foundation before embarking on the complexities of Advanced Thunder Cultivation. Do not be tempted to jump ahead!

The Exorcism By Thunder

The basic method is as follows and uses the thunder palm. It will get rid of spirits, which often feed off patients like parasites. The method is quite simple when you have mastered the thunder palm and can emit the thunder fire from your hand at will.

The patient should sit down so he or she faces you or lies down on a couch. Using cinnabar ink and a brush write the Thunder and Fire Character on your left hand. Have the patient close his eyes.

Holding your palm before the patient, let him blow a steady stream of air onto the thunder symbol painted onto your palm., meanwhile facing him you are inhaling. Then say the spell as follows:

Leigong xian chi shen guang xia zhao Difu dongjian buxiang guishen sha lu bude yincang. Ji ji ru Beiji Dadi chi!

Leigong come to us! The hand of the mighty god holding rays of light, that illuminate the mirror of the Underworld clearly the inauspicious ghosts and spirits. Reveal them and stop them!They cannot hide! Quickly by command of the Northern Pole Emperor!

Now the magician blows into the palm the patient just blew into. Ask the patient to open his eyes and describe what he can see or what part of the body the spirit seems to be attached to. If we are fortunate the patient can describe the appearance and style of clothes, colours etc, that the spirit is wearing. The magician must now talk to the Spirit and persuade it to leave. Unlike in popular fiction, the magician does not rush in guns blazing, but sets up a rapport with the spirit and finds the source of the problem. Perhaps it can be reasoned with, a deal struck and persuaded to leave.

If it leaves all is well and you can send it on its way and

perhaps even arrange offerings to it. If it does not leave and is stubborn, you will have to resort to the spirit catching method. This now follows. BUT do not use unless you have to. No one likes a bully and you are a representative of the Tao and its ambassador.

Zhuo Fa Shu
(The Skill Of Magical Capturing)

The magician forms the Five Thunder Hand Seal with his left hand, and facing the South inhales qi, visualised as dazzling light that passes to his dantian. He then utters the spell:

Wu Lei shi zhe weimeng jiang ling hong TianPili dui zhang ru yun su zhuo yaomo bu zhu xie jing, wu feng Dadi chi !

O agents of the Five Thunders descend to this place! Explosive spirit Thunderbolt of Heaven, a warrior group gathered like clouds, seize and pursue the demons and evil spirits, I request it by the Northern Emperor's command.

Now open the left hand (it's here you have gathered the Thunder power), and blow the breath at the patient's baihui point. Note that the baihui point is at the top of the head. You will see the patient suddenly tremble or shake. At this point the spirit is vulnerable and you can interrogate it. Where are you from? Why are you disturbing this person and so forth? Demand it to be truthful. Threaten to send it to Yindu, Dongyue or Chenghuang. These are different places of the afterlife.

So spirits of the deceased should be sent away into the afterlife. Demons and evil spirits are another matter altogether and must be dealt with differently. Hold the patient's left hand, when he or she inhales chant the following spell:

Wufang Lei shi da cheng weiling yunji tan suo guishen jie jing wei wu tuo suo qian qu xie jing wu feng Beiji Dadi chi !!!

Five Directional Thunder send your great spirit, converge here at this altar , the spirits and ghosts are terrified, aid me, do not neglect our request, come and remove the evil spirit here! By order of the Northern Emperor!!

Blow Qi from your mouth to the ghost Gate. Note that the ghost gates are a series of 13 points on the body. I won't list them here, you can consult any good book on acupuncture, or these days, any good acupuncture website. When this is done the Gods escort the offending spirit away.

There are other more complex methods beyond this manual, which is meant for beginners to intermediate practitioners. In the art of Maoshan Thunder. These basic methods should be cultivated first.

Introducing the Basic Thunder Symbols

There are many kinds of Thunder Symbols, which the neophyte thunder magician should learn, even before he embarks on learning other more complex and intricate forms such as those used in talismans.

The most basic is to draw a counterclockwise circle and then in the centre a tic- tac toe like pattern, or Jing character. In the middle you then write the Chi or Command character. As you are writing all this recite the following spell:

> **Tian huo lei shen Di huo lei shen, Wu Lei jiang ling suo gui guan jing Wu Di chi zhan xie mie jing. Ji ji ru luling.**

> Heavenly Fire Thunder Spirit, Earth Fire Thunder Spirit, the Five Thunders descend, the spirit locks in chains the ghosts and the spirit is guarded, by order of the Five Emperors, the evil spirits are slain by the spirit of fire. Quickly by Law!!!

> Then immediately after quietly recite:

> **Yi zhuan tian didong!**
> **Er zhuan liu shen cang.**
> **San zhuan si sha mei.**
> **Si zhuan Lei Huo sheng.**
> **Wu zhuan Pili fa.**
> **Liu zhuan shan gui si.**
> **Qi zhuan shou she yi qie ying Tian ,**

Wudao yi shiwu zhong bu zheng wei
Huo guishen bing fu Wu Lei kui,
Zhixia shou si bude dongzuo.
Ji ji ru luling!!

(With one turn the world moves, in two turns the six gods hide, in three turns and the four evils are killed, In four turns the Fire Thunder has victory, In five turns the Thunderbolt claps, In six turns the mountain ghosts are slain, In seven turns all is absorbed and meets with Heaven, That which does not follow the Dao, the fifteen types of unrighteous spirits and ghosts of misfortune and disaster are slain by the Five Thunder Lord when he acts! Quickly by command!!!!)

As you chant this spell the brush begins in the middle and then draws in a clockwise direction, seven circles, then 'shoots' out on top so you are left with a kind of tadpole shape. To the

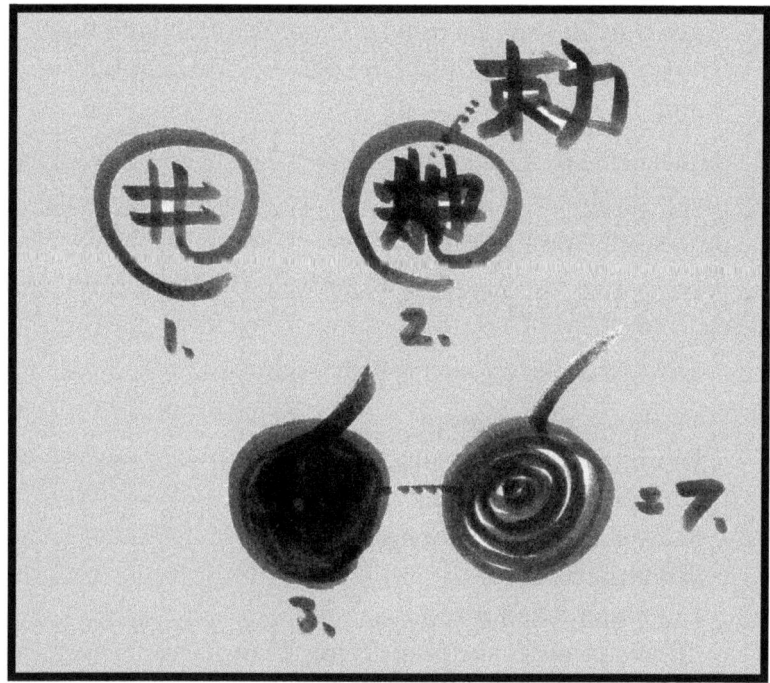

unwary, it merely looks like a blob of ink.

Like most protective and exorcistic talismans this one is best drawn on yellow paper with Chinese ink. Remember before writing it to do the thunder and lightning meditation absorbing the power from the South East and projecting the thunder power through the pen.

Steps to creating the Thunder Seal

The second type of major Thunder symbol is shown below. The process is the usual one. Go through the basic steps to assume the god form of the Thunder God as taught in the previous chapter, i.e. the lotus at the heart, the emerging of the Thunder God and your merging and becoming one with that God so there is no distinction anymore. You are then the true ambassador of the thunder powers.

Then, holding the pen visualizing the Five Thunder Gods emerging from Heaven and Earth, with clouds of crackling electrical energy and light over the pen and paper, tap the pen five times (the non-brush end) on the paper and inhale five times. Blow on the brush part of the pen and the ink-stone used for grinding the ink. Each breath should be visualized as thunder flames, with the left hand shooting flames into the visualized image of the thunder seal as you tap the paper five times. Now you can begin to write the talisman.. Begin by writing the word Thunder and then the circle with five rings.

As each loop is made you say quietly:

Yi Lei, Er Lei. San Lei, Si Lei. Wu Lei

First Thunder, Second Thunder, Third Thunder, Fourth Thunder, Fifth Thunder!!

This talisman is excellent for protection and curing illnesses, especially of the feverous type.

Five Thunder Lock Talisman

This is a variation on the first type. Drawing the tic tac toe, horizontals first and then the verticals and chanting:

> Tianhuo Lei shen, di huo lei shen, wu lei jiang ling suo gui guan jing ran ju shun shi
>
> Heavenly Thunder Fire Spirit, Earthly Thunder Fire Spirit, the Five Thunders descend and lock the ghosts and spirits and the spirits that pass this house.

As before, in a clockwise direction lock the ghosts or illness by drawing seven concentric circles and using the same chant as before:

> Yi zhuan tian didong!
> Er zhuan liu shen cang.
> San zhuan si sha mei.
> Si zhuan Lei Huo sheng.
> Wu zhuan Pili fa.
> Liu zhuan shan gui si.
> Qi zhuan shou she yi qie ying Tian,
> Wudao yi shiwu zhong bu zheng wei
> Huo guishen bing fu Wu Lei kui,
> Zhixia shou si bude dongzuo.
> Ji ji ru luling!!

With one turn the world moves, in two turns the six gods hide, in three turns and the four evils are killed, In four turns the Fire Thunder has victory, In five turns the Thunderbolt claps, In six turns the mountain ghosts are slain, In seven turns all is absorbed and meets with Heaven, That which does not follow the Dao, the fifteen types of unrighteous spirits and ghosts of misfortune and disaster are slain by the Five Thunder Lord when he acts! Quickly by command!!!!

Thunder Magick ☙ 41

You should think of the thunder shocking and shaking the Earth and the talisman image blazing with flames. This spell can exorcise or enchain spirits as well as illnesses. Occasionally it can be used to lock people in position to paralyse them.

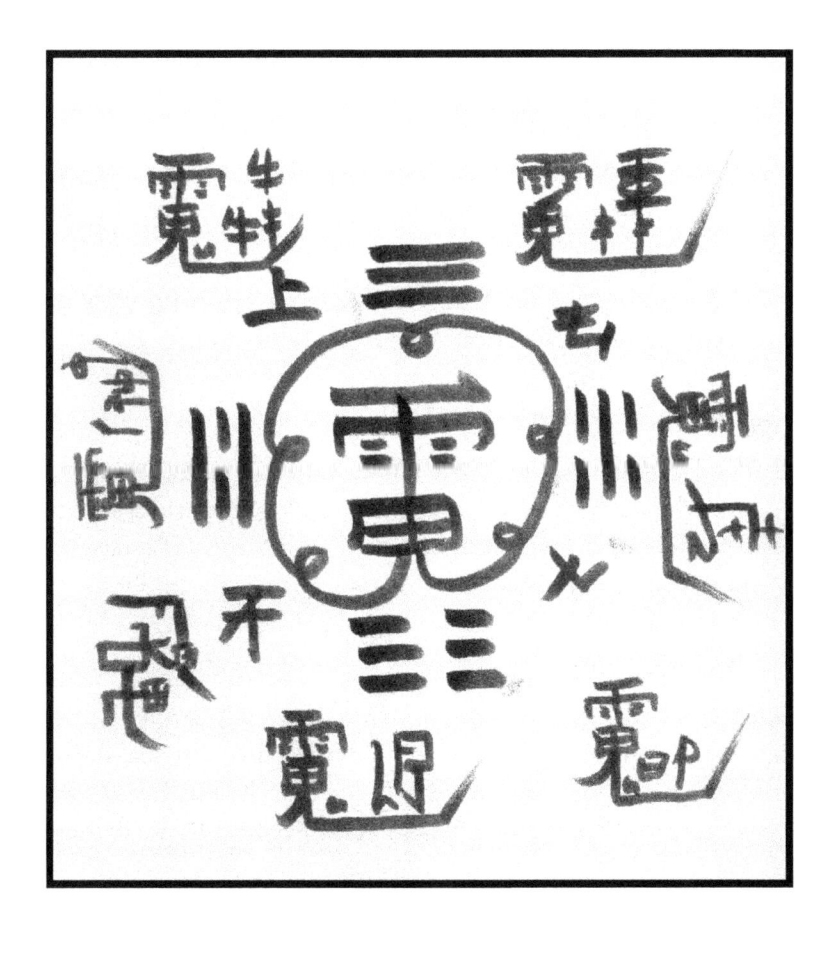

A Thunder Method To Treat Pain

There are methods to use the Thunder Power to treat pain in a patient or client as follows. Firstly it is advisable to make a special ink. Though, in my opinion it is not essential, it is highly advisable according to the Maoshan dafa, and the Masters should be trusted.

Take cinnabar (zhusha), orpiment (cihuang) and baji (this is the tuberous root of the Bietilla Hyacinth), and grind by mortar and pestle to powder and make into an ink. Use a new brush for the treatment.

On yellow paper, write the following talisman. The talisman should naturally be written on yellow paper. Yellow is auspicious and yang, so ideal for driving away evil influences. The talisman is placed on the painful area of the patient. You then breathe on the patient's painful area (remember you should have already assumed the Thunder God imagery).

Using the talisman, and by will, pull the sickness or evil spirit out of the patient with your hand in the Thunder Seal and recite the following spell:

Yi long xing yu hu hangfeng fengyu xi jibing jing gui guzi xing Wu Lei, Wu Lei Sheng xiang zhen tiankong jibing xiao baibing chu, yisheng xiang bing qing qing qihuang shendian shang qing.

The Dragon Rain and Tiger Wind, wind and rain washing away the essence of disease, ghost valley rises, the Five Thunders, the Five Thunder clap shakes the Heavens, the disease disappears, all ailments vanish as the thunder clap resounds, the disease is gone, the disease is GONE!!!

A note on invocations: I give the invocations both in English and Pinyin style Chinese. You can use either. Only proper names and actual mantric sounds are to be read in their original if you choose to recite the English form. Note that the invocations are a guide for your will and image-making faculty. To read them like it is a shopping list is useless. You must visualize all the imagery! Here follow two alternative invocations for treating ailments.

Wu Lei xiang zhen tiankong baibing sheng zhong bi qing sanhun jian qipo rong zhuque xuanwu bao anping zuo qinglong you, baihu san niu la che jibing qing fa!!

O Five Thunders shake the Heavens and all diseases are cleared! The three immortal souls and seven mortal souls . The Vermillion Bird, The Black Warrior protect and calm the left, the Green Dragon and White Tiger, three oxen pull the chariot!!!

Hua shan, shan beng, hua yao yao mie hua bing chu hua kuai kuai xiao hua zai zai mie hua pipi san hua liu cheng xue.

The mountain changes, the mountain falls, the demon, the demon is changed and extinguished, the disease changes, the disease is removed, the blockage is changed, the blockage is removed, calamity is changed, calamity is extinguished, the tumour is transformed, the tumour breaks up and becomes merely blood!

These spells should be recited three times and then focus on the patient.

Absorb the sickness qi into the talisman or hands, shout **YA!!!,** draw a cross on the ground and fling the disease qi into the cross and stamp on it. Afterwards you can, if you have the skill, give acupressure style treatment.

The Thunder Pouch

A good traditional Maoshan method is to make a yellow square thunder bag and fill with the following:(Sichuan Pepper., Wild Ginger, Notopterygium incisum, gum storax, Sweetflag, Angelica Root, Cinnabar, Chinese Clematis Root, powdered amber stone, Spatholobus spatholobi, Fructus evodiae (stinking pepper). Place the bag on the patient's wound, spot, painful area etc. The sound of thunder should be vocalised as you apply the Thunder Bag. Modern Maoshan magicians have the luxury of using recorded thunder sounds.

The Technique Of The Substitute Grass Puppet

In this technique you do not work on the patient directly but on a substitute, in this case the grass man or Cao Ren. This is made of 36 straws representing the 36 joints of the human body.. When weaving the Grass Man you must say this spell:

> **Cao Ren, Cao Ren,, hai wei kai guang bianshi cao, kai guang yihou bian shentong nu shi tang san niang nan shi wu ji sanshiliu zhi cao huazuo sanshiliu gujie dou shi shen dou shi ren.**

Grass man, grass man, you are but grass before you are opened by light, but after the light is opened, the magical power comes, the female mother, and the male warrior, the thirty six straws become the thirty-six joints and you are alive in body, a person.

It is then best to 'open' the eyes, ears, mouth and nose with cinnabar and brush. Just dab a point of cinnabar on the relevant points as you infuse life into the straw man.

Next dress it in some pieces of clothing cut from the patient's real clothes.

Place the straw man on the altar with offerings of the three meats and four fruits.

Note that the three meats are pork, beef and lamb. The three small meats are chicken, duck and fish; the four fruits are oranges, apples, melons and grapes.

Ok you now have everything ready you say the Substitute Person Spell:

Baizhi wei ni mian, wu sezhi zuo shen, xin guan bian shi zhi kai guang fu, Shen guang bing ni zuo er ting peng fu you er ting yangjian ni yu chu tongshi, tong ri, tong yue, tong nian sheng kai ni zoushou ti qian cai you shou ti jiaohuan tiqi tui chu fangwai yan xing

xing da shan yao keke dahai xing wu ke dan. Ji su zou shen bing huaji luling!!

The white paper replaces your face and the five colourered paper replaces your body. A new light opens the paper, receiving the light that duplicates magically, the light merging you together. The left ear listens to the official friend, the right ear listens to the world. You offer to simultaneously open the day and month and this year. Your left hand carries wealth and your right hand gives. Avoiding the punishments of this world, the Great Mountain restraining, the Great Sea does not punish and supports you. Quickly by Command! The Celestial Warriors come to us by command!

The magician then simply draws the fu talisman shown below and burns it. The Straw Man is now a substitute or stand in for the targeted one.

The Quick Thunder Palm Method

Provided you have cultivated the Thunder Method properly step by step, you can use this following method in an emergency, it is a very simple and quick method for arousing the Thunder Power. But it will not work unless you have put in the necessary cultivation.

Firstly draw the thunder symbol in your left palm. You can really do this with red ink and a brush...or you can simply trace it with a right sword finger into your left palm. Close your left palm into a fist and raise it above your head and recite the following spell. Remember to visualize gathering the crackling electrical energy in your palm.

OM HUNG HUNG!! Wu na wu Lei fu fa , qingtian pili yaomo su zou po xie shenfu fu dong qi Taishan Lei, Nan qi Heng Shan Lei, Xi qi Huashen Lei, Bei qi Heng Shan Bei Lei, zhong qi Gaoshan Lei, Wu Lei su fa !!!!

OM HUNG HUNG!! I raise the Five Thunder Talisman, the Thunder strikes across the clear heavens and all the evil spirits are banished. This talisman is blessed by the Gods for disintegrating evil. From the East, rise thunder of the Tai Mountain. From the South, rise Thunder from Heng Mountain, from the West, rise Thunder from Huo Mountain,from the North rise thunder from Heng Northern Mountain, from the centre rise Gaoshan Thunder!! The Five Thunders strike instantly!!

Now release the fist into an open palm suddenly as if throwing a stone saying the mantra **OM HUNG HUNG** at the target.

Five Thunder Talismans

The Five Thunder Talismans are a popular form of Taoist magic found in most schools, including Maoshan.

They are extremely protective and can be placed in your home, carried or even burnt and the ashes mixed in water and drunk. The effect is to build thunder power in your organism, which will go a long way to helping you in the processes of the Thunder 'yoga'.

Naturally you should follow all the steps of assuming the Thunder God form as given in the basic cultivation technique. When you swallow such 'Thunder Water' focus on absorbing that power and storing it in the dantian.

Here is a useful spell used for consecrating and empowering the thunder talismans and then some examples of five thunder talismans for your own usage.

1. Wu Lei Zhou
(Five Thunder Spell)

Wu jin qing, Wu Lei dajiangjun jiaota qi xing, Wu Lei lun sheng jia , Wu Lei da pusa jiangluo fanjian jiu tiangmin zhi xie zhan gui sha you jing bai qing Wu Lei dajiangjun fanjian fuzhu dizi (name of person) shou xie zhan gui jin miewang Leigong ,Lei Mu, daojia tang shen bing huoji ni luling!!!

With five sincere requests I invoke the Five Thunder Generals, travelling by the Seven Stars, the Five Thunders Masterly chariot, the Five Thunders Great Deity descends to the world of the mortals to rescue the good people, to cure ills and exorcise unhealthy influences and slay the ghosts , the great spirit which we pay courtesy towards, we request the Five Thunders Generals to descend to the mortal realm to support the daoist disciple (name) and to rid of the evil influences and slay the ghosts ... to drain them and to extinguish them. Leigong, Leimu (the Thunder Mother), O perfected and excellent Gods, the warriors rush here like fire by command!!!

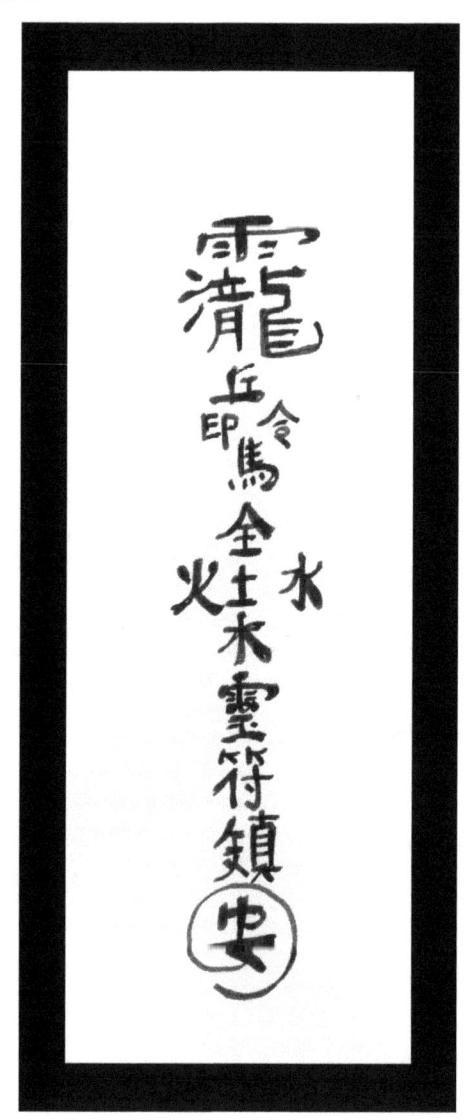

Five Thunder Talisman

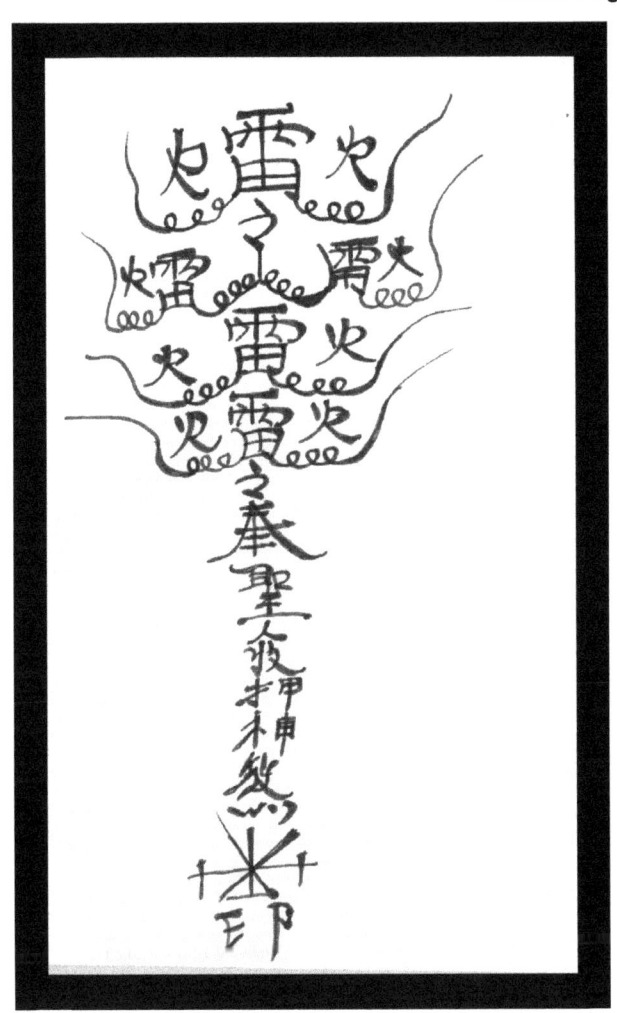

Thunder Magick 51

Five Thunder Talisman (another)

Five Thunder Talisman (another)

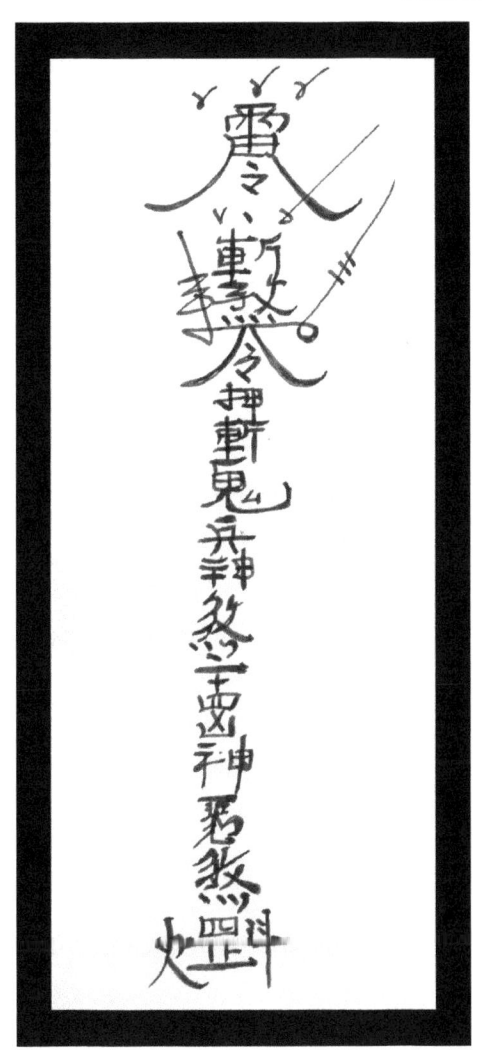

Thunder Magick ☙ 53

Five Thunder Talisman (another)

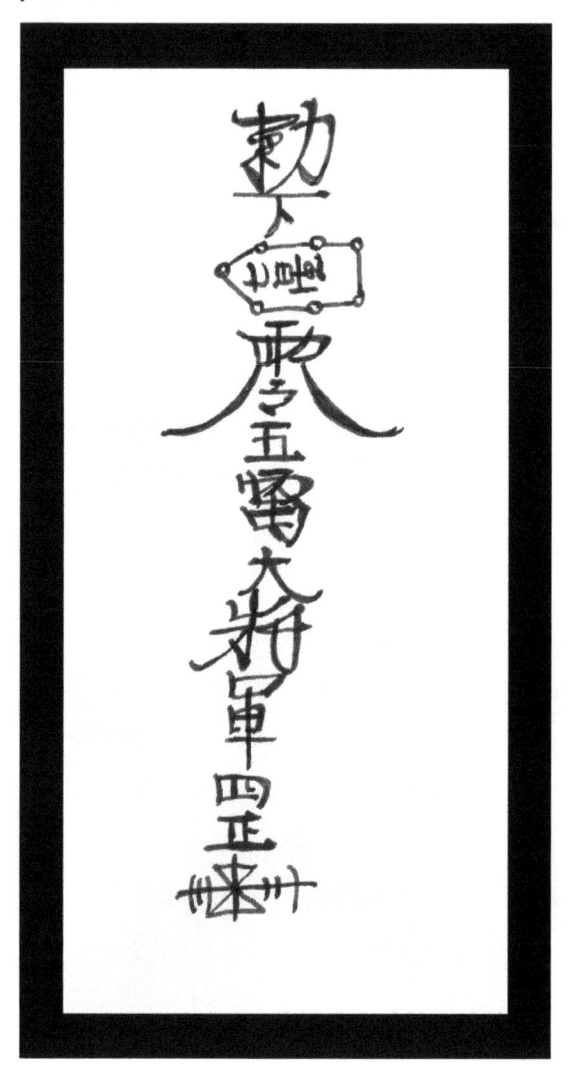

Five Thunder Talisman (another)

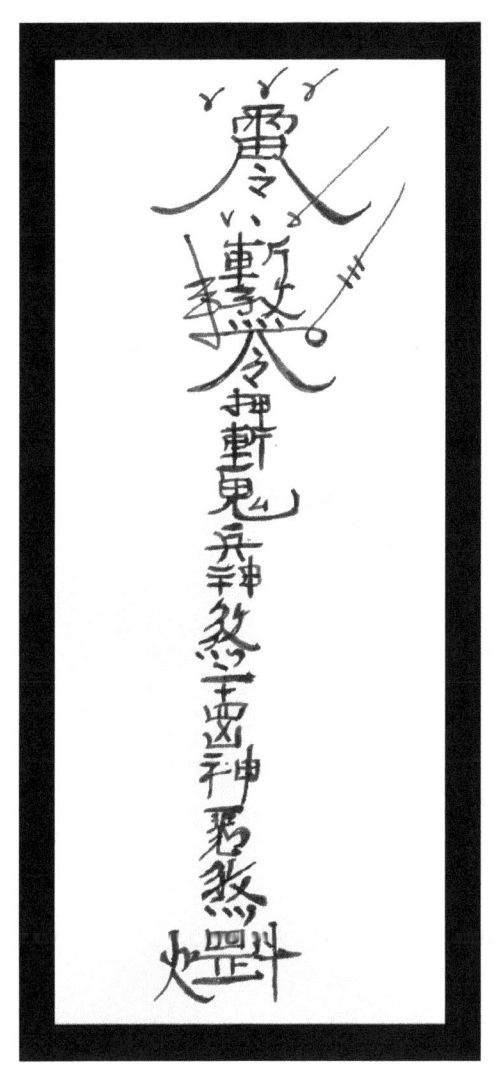

Thunder Magick ◌ 55

Five Thunder Talisman (another)

Five Thunder Talisman (another)

Thunder Magick ☙ 57

Five Thunder Talisman (another)

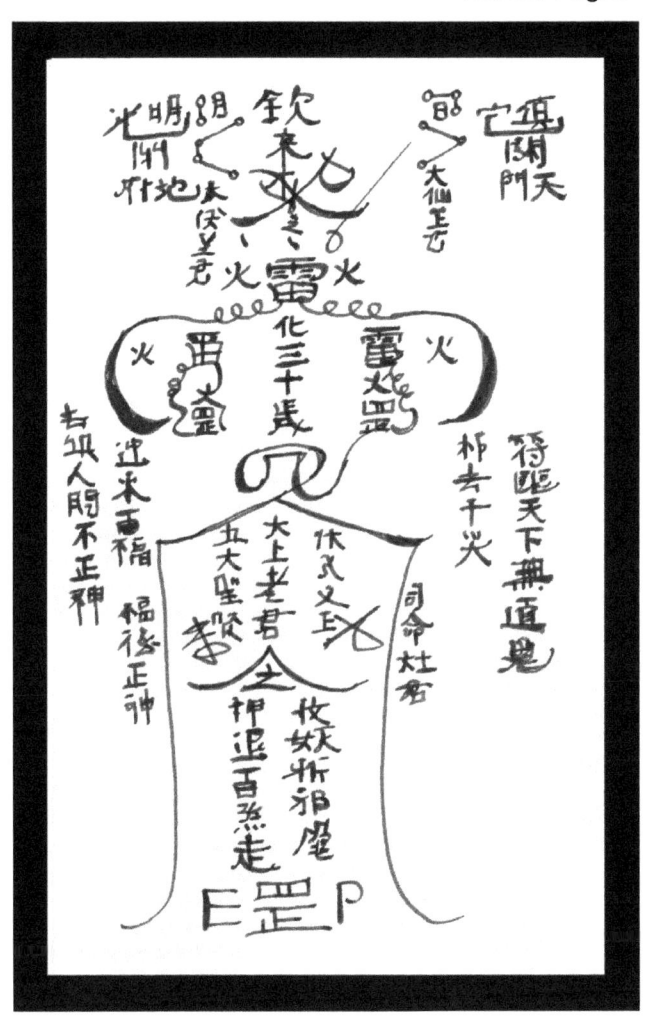

The Fire Of The Five Thunders Or The So Called Samadhi Fire

We now reach the final section of our basic introduction and cultivation of the Five Thunder magic of the Maoshan school.

I should point out there is much more to learn and these will be covered in future booklets or even a book. There is enough in this small manual to master the fundamentals.

The Thunder alchemy involving even more complex visualizations and the use of the five internal organs is a topic that requires a manual by itself.

What now follows is a spell that once you cultivate is very dangerous. This spell can be used to cleanse entire rooms or houses of unhealthy areas and even plagues.

However, it can also be used to manifest real fire that can burn people and things. Masters can even use it to punish evildoers. This was called 'Sending the Fire'. The recipient for example, may receive a mysterious package or parcel. On opening it, all they would see are some burnt clothes and ashes. They have just been sent the fire.

When you have cultivated this method you can practice manifesting this power via flammable substances ... for example, a cup of petrol or similar flammables.

The spell requires three talismans as shown below.

The altar is set up with a red altar cloth and red candles, incense etc. In this case though, do not have the bowl of water.

The invocation is said and then the talismans burned to ashes. The ashes are spread through the place to be cleansed by spiritual Thunder Fire or sent as a package with the talismanic ashes and singed clothes to the target, though this is not essential.

The samadhi fire is one of the most dreaded of the Thunder spells

The Samadhi Fire Spell

Shi bushi feifan shen wo shi Nanfeng Bingding shen jinri chu dong wu bie shi shao diao sishi hua huichen shou nei tiqi Wu Lei Huo shi qi Lei Huo mantian hong rao de san wuchu bi qian shen ran nan tao ming you tianran kai disha di yin shen lu da jiang wufang jia qi wu Lei Huo sishi jia zai dangxin zhong xian lu guamu hou liu yi gu hu liu zai yibian cun wufeng Lei Huo chong jian. Ji Ji Ru Luling!!!!

I, the Master of Spells is not a God, but today I am the Southern God of Fire. When you soar from the hidden cave, burning the corpses and transforming them to mere dust and ash. From your hand comes the Five Thunder Fire!!

O the Thunder and the Fire transforms the heavens from white to red. Mercy and the three righteousnesses are nowhere to be seen, a thousand gods cannot help you flee for your life, the earth opens up and the Lord of the Earth and the Evil Star cries aloud at the journey of the Fire God!!!

The Five Directions rise, The Five Thunder Fire burns the Corpses, staying in the midst, only the coffins and bones remain.

By the Five Thunder Fire soaring from Heaven!!! Quickly by Law!

Samadhi One

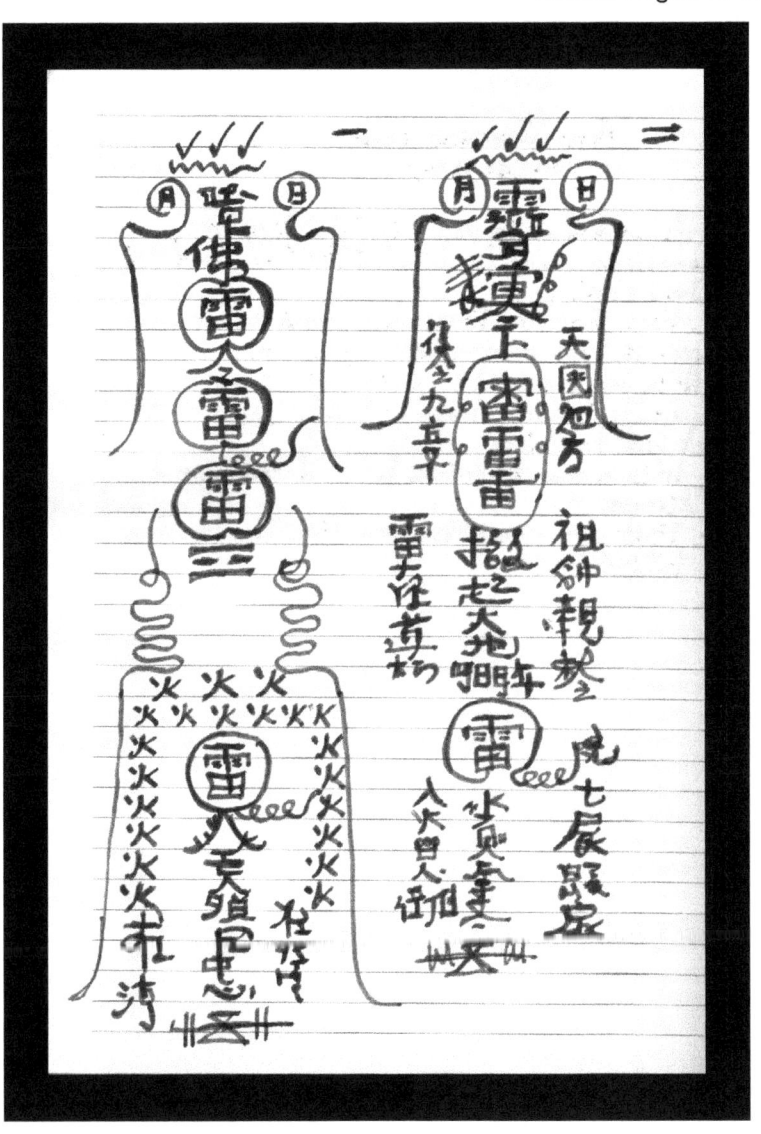

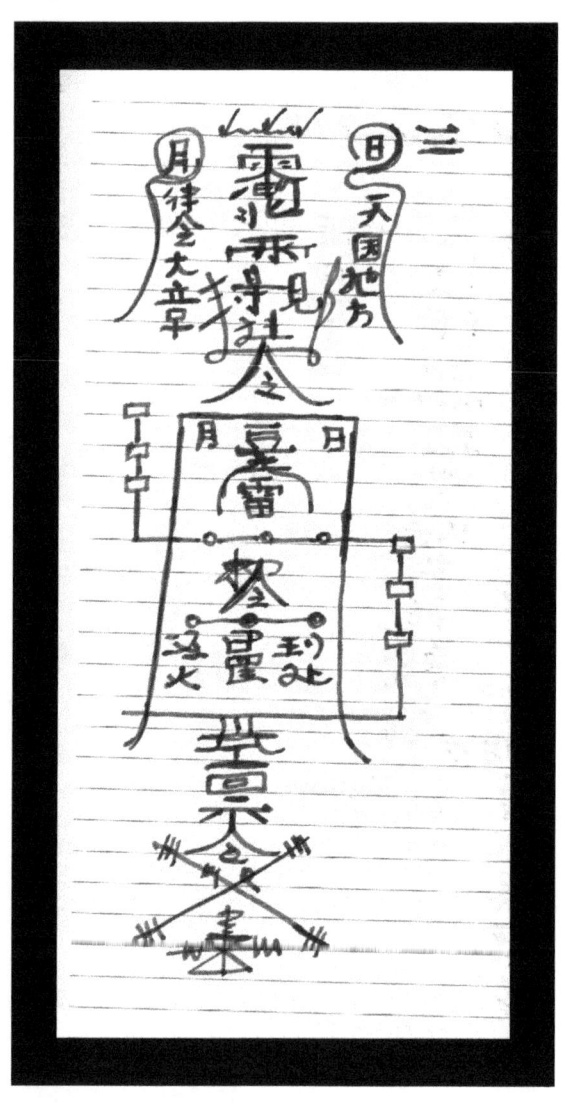

Samadhi Two

Glossary

BAI YU CHAN. One of the founders of the Thunder magic tradition.

CINNABAR. A red pigment derived from nature composed of mercury and sulphur. It is often used in Chinese alchemy, medicine and magic. However it is poisonous in nature.

CAI JU LEI DAN FA. A method of gathering thunder chi from the local atmosphere during a storm. Really a specialised form of qigong.

DANTIAN. A point of major importance in Chinese yoga and medicine. It is located about two finger widths below the navel. It is considered a storage point for occult energies and particularly of jing qi...the sexual fires.

DINGZI. A Yang day in the Chinese calendar. This can be ascertained by an almanac or a simple app. It is named for any of the six yin **EARTHLY BRANCHES.**

DINGZI BU. A stance adopted in Taoist conjuration and said to be passed down from the magician king Yu the Great. It is a t shaped stance, or the character ding. The left foot is forward pointing and the left heel is placed in the instep of the right foot. The right foot toes are pointing to the sides.

DRAGON BOAT FESTIVAL. A major festival of the Chinese

ritual calendar that occurs on the fifth day of the fifth lunar month. It is an auspicious day sacred to the dragon.

EARTHLY BRANCHES. The twelve Earthly Branches are used in representing time along with the Heavenly Stems. Their most familiar representation are the twelve animals of the Chinese 'zodiac', beginning with the Rat. As hours, each branch has two hours assigned to it. Each hour has its own specific magical properties.

FIVE THUNDERS. The generic name of a specific kind of magic that uses five kinds of heavenly essences or energies that correspond to the five elements of Chinese metaphysics...Earth, Fire, Wood, Metal and Water.

FA GONG. Method skill, a skill in magic similar to siddhi in Tantric thought.

JIAZI. A Yin day.

JING SHINEI. A room set aside for the cultivation of meditation and magic.

LAO ZI. The mysterious philosopher and mystic who wrote the Dao de Jing before disappearing into the West. He is considered the founder of Taoism. But in Taoist thought, Lao Zi was just one of the avatars of a greater spiritual impulse. See **Taishang Laojun.**

LEI FA. The thunder method. The method and cultivation of thunder magic.

LEI GONG. The most well known of the thunder gods. He is shown as a man with wild hair and a bird's feet and claws and a beak. Sometimes with wings.

MAOBI. The Chinese brush pen.

MAOSHAN. One of the great schools of occultism and practical magic in China and in Chinese communities throughout Asia. It should not be confused with Maoshan Orthodoxy represented by the Shanqing school which is a philosophical Taoist school that also originated from Maoshan Mountain. Scholars believe that Maoshan as a sorcery school originated in Sichuan among the many shamanic folk practices of the indigenous people.

MARSHAL PENG. One of the chief thunder deities of the Taoist pantheon. He is the master and commander of the Thunder Bureau in Heaven. His most striking feature is his gleaming silver teeth.

SAMADHI FIRE. A kind of spiritual fire energy conjured in certain rites to sweep evil away and in times of war, the enemy. Samadhi is the sanskrit name for a certain state of consciousness that can obliterate the ego, hence the name.

SAN QING. The Three Pure Ones. The highest beings in Taoism that caused or helped in the manifestation of the cosmos and in the spiritual evolution of mankind.

SIFU/SHIFU. A master. The Taoist equivalent of a Guru.

TAI CHI the Great Ultimate. The first point of manifestation from the unknown negative existence of Wu Ji. We could compare it to Kether in Qabalistic thought.

TAISHANG LAOJUN. One of the Three Pure Ones whose function is to help mankind in his spiritual evolution. His best known incarnation was Lao Zi.

TUNYAN. To swallow, absorb energy.

WUZANG. The five so called hard organs in the body that are associated with the five elements.
Wood with liver. Fire with the heart. Earth with the spleen. Metal with the lungs and Water with the kidneys.

XIE. Unhealthy environmental Qi or energy that can come from negative spirits, people, places and astrological factors.

ZHEN. The trigram that represents Thunder in the I Jing.

ZHUSHA. Chinese cinnabar ink.

Ingram Content Group UK Ltd.
Milton Keynes UK
UKHW020608120523
421633UK00011B/377